GREASY HANDSHAKES

GREASY HANDSHAKES

Richard Gegick

WPA Press
Pitcairn, PA 15140

For Jimmy Vaccaro, the famous Las Vegas bookmaker from Trafford. The action in our hearts is always on home.

"Look at your waiter's face. He knows."
-Anthony Bourdain

"I might not finish this shift, but I'll finish this bottle of wine."
-Ed Wolf

East Pittsburgh Collapse

The PennDot representative
wearing a white hard hat said
Rt. 30 caved in due to March rain,
and that's true, maybe, but it felt
like a lie. The ground under the pavement
has been soft for years, mushy
as rotten pear flesh, the muck sucking
tennis shoes and wingtips and flip-flops
and crocs, steel-toed boots.
The reporters didn't bother with
any real questions like how many
Budweiser six pack rings does it take
to catch a carp in Turtle Creek?
How many Vicodin does it take
to make a major highway slide down a hill?

1

PART ONE

Garden

My father's postage-stamp garden sits off the front porch.
He grows green beans, tomatoes, carrots,
hot peppers that hang like fat, bent fingers.
He fertilizes the tired soil with blue-gill heads,
the innards of gutted trout come spring.
When I was a child he let me plant watermelon seeds;
one swelled on the vine like magic.
I never inherited his ability to make things grow
like the backyard where he shows me the zucchini,
the pumpkin blossoms the color of taffy.
Vines stretch across rocks, broken glass.
When a car pulls up to the house behind us and a man
rises from it like a ghoul from a rusty crypt
my father says, "That's a heroin house."

"I could never raise you kids in this town, now."

But the man knocking on his dealer's door is about my age
and like me he already grew up here.

The Lunch Regular Shits His Pants

Five minutes after you
take his order, he
waves you down, says
he's ready to order.

You tell him he
already ordered and
he says,
"I want a turkey sandwich."

The average guest-age
in this restaurant is
deceased. Christ.

This ancient man comes
in every single weekday,
and the routine never
changes.

Ginger ale, turkey sandwich,
cup of decaf, shits his pants.

You'd feel sorry for the
decrepit bastard, but
you don't have time.

The crones on 206 need
cappuccino and the young
couple sitting patio,

drinking martinis, need
to know if the calamari
is gluten free.

So you let him sit
in his booth with
crapped pants.

You run his black Amex,
call his aide, froth the milk,
and grab a mop.

The Lunch Regular's Granddaughter

On lunch shifts my brains are in my pockets,
useless dryer lint, a handful of coins.
It's loving the way she feeds him gazpacho,
daubs his chin clean with a linen napkin,
clears space between tables for his walker
so he can make his way to the bathroom.
With one of his elderly friends he drinks
cranberry juice, iced tea, ginger ale.
With his granddaughter it's always wine
and he turns delirious with it,
lifts his head from his chest and smiles
at the wait staff, the managers, other guests
like he's been touched by the hand of God.

Maybe he has because on these days
when I approach the table I can smell her hair,
and I swear it smells like peach pie,
her engagement ring a piece of hard candy,
and I know what those old clergymen
talk about when they claim to feel the Holy Spirit
breathe or move about their rooms, vestibules.
I can feel it, too. The Holy Spirit is a woman.
The Holy Spirit is a chicken salad sandwich,
no bun, that I serve her for lunch,
I can find it anywhere on these shifts
when she dines with her grandfather.
Even, most miraculously, in myself.

To Bailey, Who's Name Is Written On The Side Of A Train

God knows where these tracks lead.
I've lived here all my life and still don't know.
Mysteries hide in these valley towns
like the neighborhood behind the Wolvarena.
Most of the houses are for sale, and I hope
a kind and merciful God raptured the people
who lived here to a heaven where the fridge is always full
of beer, where the children never break their popsicles in half.
I wonder, Bailey, if you see the train car on your way to Aldi,
or on your way to pick up a pack of smokes, or driving
to the bar where you pump dollar bills into a Cherry Master
and drink cheap rum with canned Pepsi, digging a hole
into another afternoon, another sunset you'll miss.
It's another tripwire, they are everywhere here,
buried deep in the brush of our hearts, waiting to be run through
and blow us all to bits. You're lucky, Bailey.
Someone thought you were one hell of a woman
to pull that stunt, to dot the 'i' with a heart, even if only
for a little while. I've no doubt they were right.

Wyoming
for John Cazale

She's right, I think. Partially.
We're all sad. Men and women.
Everyone else on the spectrum.
Gender doesn't matter.
If we're not sad what are
we doing sneaking around
neighborhoods where nobody
will know either of us?

Funny how I've spent my life
with escape plans in my pocket.
She should've seen me
tear up the back roads in that
rusted out Ford sedan,
the engine full of sludge.
I thought I was born to run,
though I always turned back
when I reached the highway.

We're all Sal in that old movie,
Dog Day Afternoon,
when he discovers the one place
he'd like to go isn't possible
because Wyoming isn't a country.
That's us this afternoon.
Our eyelids droop,
our spines are stiff,
our guns cocked and loaded
waiting for what never comes.

The Ocean

Tony's cooked here since
the renewal center
over a decade ago.

Twice a GED failure, he barely reads,
but knows how to cook a steak, how to
work hard, show up on time.

His roommate, Daryl, is dying of cirrhosis.
They were cell mates in the pen,
rumored lovers.

I went to their apartment once,
and they slept on bunk beds like jail,
Daryl was top.

Now Tony drives after endless ticket
Saturdays to spend the night bedside
at Cleveland Clinic.

The late-night highway air soothes
grease burned arms and hands covered
with blisters.

Sundays he drives all morning to
make it back for the early
dinner rush.

During pre-shift I ask how Daryl
is doing in Cleveland though I
already know.

"Not good," he says. "But at
least while I was up there I finally
got to see the ocean."

The Morning News

Last month some kid got shot
outside my bedroom window.
The bullets angry wasps,
I heard them cut the air
before the crack of gun.
I hit the floor,
stayed there with my hands
over my head as I was taught
to do in bomb and tornado drills
as the kid, 23, cried for help.
Stayed there until minutes
later the screaming stopped
and he was finally dead.
That's when I looked out,
saw the neighboring houses
light up simultaneously.
All of us amazed at what the body does
before the mind.

Chewed Fingernails

If I am impoverished, let me remain in poverty
whistling sad tunes under train trestles with empty pockets.
If I am soulless, do not bless my forehead with your fingers.
If I am alone, do not let my name slip from your lips
or rest on the your wine stained tongue like gossip.
If I am silent, do not engage me in conversation,
more than likely I am tuned in on those trains,

the ones I can hear without tracks nearby,
carrying a load of coal, can pick them up
like a Mets broadcast on a clear night,
their sound coming to me in coffee shops, restaurants,
bars where the jukebox blows all the
the misses of the previous five decades,
where the hearts of the old men barely pump,

sounding so close I could lay a penny down
for the steel wheels to stretch like taffy,
so close I could hop a boxcar in a Kerouac wet dream
where cowardice transforms into bravery,
where fate and responsibility are fingernails
chewed off and spit to the floor in anxious moments.

Worse Than Weed Dreams

Like this one I had where the restaurant
was an airplane hangar

and I couldn't see where the tables ended
just an ocean of white linen

The only waiter on staff and all I did
was run and pour and serve

the last thing I remember was desperately
needing a shrimp cocktail

Or the other one I had where the whole
dining room was seated

At each table were members of my family
mother, father, aunts, uncles

and I was the only server again
while they ran me ragged

But the worst are the dreams where
nothing special happens

just a repetition of a normal shift
waiting tables

and I wake realizing there's no escape

Hailing a Cab, 2 A.M. Downtown

In Pittsburgh they just roll by.
When they pass
through the traffic light
I am nothing but a ghost
waving my hands, yelling,
on the street corner of Limbo.

Women in Pittsburgh

kick you out in the dark amid an April
snowstorm because they don't do sleepovers.
You leave feeling like a miracle in reverse,
not believing the snow
laying an inch thick on the sidewalk,
lost in a suburb where the
houses look the same and the road
you drive doesn't take you to the highway,
but dips down to the empty pool.
You park there by the concrete canyon,
wait for sunrise, hoping its light
will guide you to your bedroom where you
pull the blinds down and ignore it
for the rest of the day.

Bob's Lounge
For Pajich, again

You once wrote you can't
understand why you keep going.
It's true the place
looks like Styrafoam cup
filled with tobacco spit.

Let's be honest.
We both go because the beer
is cheap, so are the wings.
We go because we're addicted
to the black eyes,
chipped teeth, the sinister
heartbeat of the billion
domestic police calls
all through these towns.

We go because we're frauds,
unable to find comfort
in the fancy corridors,
unable to find it here
where if the man across the bar
knew our thoughts he'd
brain us with a hammer.

You wrote you are afraid
of everyone here.
Really we're only afraid of
how much we love
this place without it
ever loving us back.

Pittsburgh

On any night someone will play The Skyliners.
I can't tell what year it is,
though I know I am in Pittsburgh.
My Pittsburgh. A jar of pickled eggs.
A losing bingo card in my pocket.
A reminder of a world how I want it,
an ideal, the smell of kielbasa and kraut
on Steelers Sunday, a memory of a time
I am not sure ever really existed.
In this city it's impossible to know
whether I'm glorifying someone else's past
or living my own future.

Poem for Elvis on his Birthday

I've put aluminum foil on my windows,
blocked all sunlight, crawled inside myself,
found nothing but used condoms,
buckets full of half-eaten fried chicken bones,
red ink delinquency notices, my credit score
hidden under my pillow like a pistol,

the skin of lost lovers gathered in the corner of my room,
the hair nests of new ones tangled in bed sheets
freshly soiled with perfume and semen.

Was this your Graceland, Elvis?
The most famous man in the world isolated
from sunlight, cocooned in Dilaudid,
who wandered into his long dead mother's
walk-in closet full of her coats,
wrapped himself in them just to smell her.

I searched for you tonight, Elvis,
and couldn't find you anywhere.

A Real Job

People love to talk shit when servers complain
about low wages, lack of health care and sick days,
getting stiffed on tips,

they say if we don't like it
we should find a real job,

as if jobs with health care, vacation days,
and a 401k grow like dandelions
in derelict mill-town front yards,

as if what we do for money is fake.

The wine glass stem I jammed through
my palm was real. So was the blood
the color of Barolo, brick-red,
that dripped onto the white linen table cloth.
So was the car ride to the ER
napkin wrapped around the wound.

The money lost to an afternoon spent
waiting to get stitched up was real,
and I'll never get that money back.

After her shift, this waitress I know
stopped by and coated my
five stitches with anti-biotic cream.

Her fingers felt real as anything.

Rocks

She wears rocks in her bra
gemstones and crystals polished smooth
to bring love and openness, calm
and peace, good fortune, and the short
shot of wealth during a Saturday night shift

and when I unhook it
they slide down her freckled breasts
into the sheets, where in the afternoon
sun
they reflect a kaleidoscope
on her face

and I drift up
like a child's wayward balloon
into the cloudless sky.

To-Go

I never bother to call ahead for food,
instead employ the old mill-hunk trick
to steal an hour alone.
I say, "I'll go get it,"
then drink at the makeshift three stool
bars of Chinese restaurants
where dust coats the liquor bottles,
and the person who works the phone
eyes me suspiciously because
I am the only person drinking there.

When I return home a little buzzed
with a bag full of sweet and sour pork,
egg rolls, lo mein, there is music,
a wine bottle open, a woman on my couch
wearing blue wool socks,
and I drop like a handful of loose change.
I say things like, "I love you,"
though I'm never sure if I mean them.

Wellbutrin

The doctor says if I'm serious
about quitting smoking he can
prescribe me Wellbutrin,
it assists the addiction and will
help with my depression.

Sometimes there is no God.
Sometimes there is a God of mercy.

Today I walk in His light
because I do not have the genital warts
I'd feared, no STD. I am healthy,
maybe not pure, but close enough.

I decline the prescription.
The posters of smoker's lungs
the color and shape of a worn
catcher's mitt hang in the office.
They are a warning for the inevitable
moments when God disappears,
and I am left to wonder
whether He'll show his face again.

PART TWO

Polish Hill

Up here Champagne flutes shatter
on the pavement early mornings.

The sky still dark, birds clamor for the sun.

Up here, homeless cats loiter on porches,
waiting for food, affectionate hands.

Up here is the index finger of the city,
tapping our chests to make its point,

and on the concrete stairs
we tie our strings together so tight
there will be no choice later but to cut them.

Jimmy Is Doing Heroin Now

He panhandles in the kitchen, hitting up
servers for a buck or two, saying he's
a little short, needs lunch money
for his kids and bus fare home. I remember
when his second daughter was born,
how the whole staff signed a card and gave cash
for diapers and formula,
to relieve some of the burden that comes
when two people drag a child into this world.

Yesterday, I watched him nod off as he whisked
a batch of chocolate mousse. It was almost funny
the way his head dipped to his chest but his
arm kept swinging through the whipped egg whites,
the chunks of chocolate. But it wasn't funny.
Today he's looking for cash to score so I slip
him a twenty. He's pulled me out of the weeds
so many times, put my forgotten soufflé
on the fly, jumped my tickets to the front.
It's the least I can do, even if the only fucked
up thing I can do for my friend is keep him
from getting dope sick on the job.

Soon as I give him the cash he bolts from
his station, the half chopped tomatoes on the board,
to hit up his man stationed downtown.
Soon as he's gone I miss him, even though today
I know he'll return. One day soon he won't.
Jimmy will end up in jail or die.

Robber Baron Heart

Don't let people fool you,
the academics in high-back booths
who sip whisky and sew
Marxist theory like a patchwork quilt.
Or the posturing socialist
gutter poets and band freaks
who guzzle beer in rotten molar
dive bars glued on these hills.
We are all born with a second heart
hidden behind the first,
buried in the holes of our gut
like old porno magazines.

I hear it beat Saturday nights,
my section full of hissing diners
whose wine glasses are empty,
who wait for their craft cocktails
to be crafted by apathetic bartenders,
who have half an hour until
their show and not yet served dinner,
who have been served filet
medium-well ordered medium-rare.

Their faces turn to fists
as they calculate money spent
over services received.
Though I've no control over variables
I remain the equation's constant,
and I make bargains with God,
lick the Devil's wingtips,
offer my soul to any Hindu deity,
plead with the cosmos
for a twenty percent tip.

We are all born capitalists,
all born with the secret hearts
of robber barons bent on murder,
willing to maim, cripple,
flood entire towns for pleasure,
our desires, our good times.
Don't let anyone fool you.
Touch it. Feel it pump.

The New Hostesses

One day in the past two years
I crossed a border.
No Checkpoint Charlie
there to greet me,
no demarcation or wall.
I am *older.*
Any opportunity
for a workplace romance
these days feels less
than life affirming and more
like a boat taking on water.
Besides, I am invisible
to the hostesses now,
they no longer so much
as acknowledge me
during pre-shift cigarettes,
and I'm not welcome
in the coat closet mid-shift.
Still, I watch them
at the front desk running
this restaurant,
my puppet strings
tied around their fingers,
and I am reminded of those
days still so recent
when it was too easy
to fall in love.

Moons Over My-Hammy

Across the highway from the North Versailles K-Mart
is a Denny's where the waitresses hate their jobs
as much as they hate their husbands and children.

They hate the teenage couples eating ice cream
after second-run movie dates and stale popcorn,
the girls in sweatpants, the boys in sweatpants,
all of them fat — everyone here is fat.

Hate the people who walk out on Grand Slam checks,
the cosmic bowlers who've had one too many
and grope at their green polyester uniforms,
the neighborhood kids who sit all night

kids like me who claimed those booths for hours
smoking cigarettes and drinking coffee,
constantly asking for refills because there
was never anything better to do
except maybe fool around in the Foodland parking lot.

The waitresses drink Pepsi and orange juice in
the server alley until their tongues blossom
with ulcers. You hear them talk about their husbands.

"I told him if he ordered
Domino's again I'd cut his dick off. I mean,
how hard is it for that dumb cocksucker
to boil a pot of water and open a jar?"

I am here now waiting on an oil change,
because I have a gift card to blow,
and am bored, hungry, and lonely
as anyone at two in the afternoon.
I know these waitresses hate me, too.
When I'm in this town,
hate feels just as good as love.

Cash Hardens the Hearts of Waiters

When gas company executives,
slick haired and smelling of cologne,
sit in my section and order
five-hundred-dollar bottles of wine,
whole Maine lobsters as appetizers,
sixty-dollar steaks thicker than paving bricks
cooked medium rare, soufflé for desert
with snifters of amber colored cognac,
X.O. sold at ninety dollars an ounce,
I no longer care about poison fracking solution
pumped into the ground, don't care
about big river fish kills in West Virginia
where smallmouth bass float belly up
like condoms and beer cans in polluted water,
don't care about the earthquakes in Ohio,
the Youngstown homes that trembled.

My only care is the gratuity line,
twenty percent of 2,000 dollars so this month
I can grocery shop at Trader Joe's
for fresh produce, wild caught salmon,
Swiss chocolate bars pocked with hazelnuts.
Ever grocery shop at Family Dollar?
Walk the aisles that look tornadoed,
splintered and trashed for Bisquick,
jarred pasta sauce so sugary
it tastes like candy, blisters the tongue?
Every step on the gray tile
is a reminder of your own poverty.
But not this week. No, I'll buy food
that's real and wholesome,
maybe with enough money left
to take the cut on a Wednesday night.

Wayne Says

He says it doesn't matter what
it says on my diploma,
how many hours I've spent
in workshops
dull as unsalted butter
saying things like,

"What's at stake in this story?"

"The protagonist's motivation
is not clear in this piece."

"This relies too heavily
on flashback, needs more
base-time action."

Doesn't matter how many
nights I've spent post workshop
where myself and the rest
posture and pose
as the serious people
we want the world to think
we are, chain smoking
trading Vonnegut, Roth,
Hempel, Whitehead,
debating whether David Foster Wallace
is a genius or a fraud
in those hard wooden
Squirrel Cage booths.

I always said fraud
but like all of us
the truth is it's both.

I am no genius,
but it's like Wayne says:
No matter where I go
or the friends I make,
the magazines I publish in,

in my heart
I will always be scum from Trafford.

Babushkas

In high school I pumped gas on college football Saturdays, lifted the hoods of Buicks, Pintos, AMC Eagle hatchbacks built like tanks with wood paneling on the sides, for the babushkas, the old ladies who never used self-serve a day in their lives, who held families together with kitchen twine and cabbage, with wooden spoons on the asses of mouthy children, with money stashed in Folger's cans under sinks so their husbands wouldn't blow it on beers at the Polish Club, back room poker games.

After I'd fill the tank, check the oil, the transmission fluid, the coolant, power-steering, brake fluid, tire pressure, they'd take fifty-cents of hidden money and press two quarters into my palm with their twisted fingers, tell me what a good a boy I was, implore me to get a coffee or maybe a hamburger from the Burger King across the street, even though I got all the free coffee I wanted and back then a Whopper still cost two dollars.

Ray, September 1983

In the picture of him at my parents' backyard
shotgun wedding he salutes the camera with a can
of Stroh's beer and a Camel between his fingers.

The white carnation in his lapel matches the paper
streamers decorating the above ground pool and
he is happy as any Slovak can be, half-smiling.

Behind him the Tiki lights on the toolshed bar
burn through early evening mill sulfur haze
like horrible and doomed constellations.

To My Friend Who Drinks Vodka for Breakfast

Our fathers were terrible gamblers.
They bet on the Bills four years in a row,
still owe money to pizza parlor bookies.
They were all Bill Buckners for whom
money was a routine grounder trickling
under their glove, between their legs.
They maxed out all the credit cards,
skated on bar tabs, dug themselves
a grave one Budweiser at a time.

All of this, friend, is our only inheritance,
their debts become our debts.

The collectors will come—
Only so many times you can turn
the lights off and pretend you're not home.
You can hide your heart in a cheap
fifth or a handle like a car parked
in the woods or at a cousin's house
two towns over trying to avoid repo.
They will always find it and haul
it away on a flatbed while you sleep.
Unfair but we all have to pay,
and brother with the way your hands
shake there isn't much time to get square.
Won't be long now until they
take everything you love.

A Couple Beers

A couple beers on an empty stomach
and I'll eat anything, even the tuna noodle casserole
my poor mother used to make with crumbled
potato chips on top. I swore never to eat it
after I left home, but then there are the beers.
Things I'd never do become the things I *might* never do.
No answer to what came first, beer or desperation.
All the bars know the answer doesn't matter.
Desperation is a house plant turning sunlight
into sugar, it's the mortar in a brick wall,
the varicose veins of an old barber.
It's one more beer ordered when
I've already had enough, hoping in the time
it takes to drink something might happen.

Promised Land
For Bruce

I've been thinking about tornadoes,
their random violence and odd precision,
how they dip from the sky
and splinter one house to matchsticks
but leave another unscathed,
a busted window or two,
a rain gutter ripped off.

I want to turn into one.
I want to spit hailstones, shit lightning,
my thunder voice bellowing out
as I cut my path down the city blocks,

descend from a black-lung sky,
blow away all the hatred and disgust and deception,
snap the heartbreak and sorrow and longing
like telephone poles and tree branches.

I'm a man, I'm a man,
goddamn it all, I'm a man.

Five and a Half Games Back, Last Week of September

Another season almost gone.
A hurricane's remnants flash
gutters to rapids, streets to rivers,
sweep up dumpsters,
cars, uprooted trees, beer cans.
We've turned cold,
a bi-polar mood swing of weather,
and I long for the mathematical
possibilities of early June
where I spent at least one day
in first place, where the next start
could be the start of a ten game streak.

There is always hope
until there is none and now

the daily box scores are no longer
a road map to joy.
They are the crow flying
to the inevitable conclusion,
October's ash tray skies.
Until week's end I am stuck in
this purgatory of too many losses,
too few wins. My hands still
reach for the pennant's fire,
and if I someday touch it,
I have enough fuel to burn forever.

The Power of Now

I've read all those books, too.
The self-help ones
about living in the now,
the present.

Most nights I feel
like I'm an overstuffed
filing cabinet. My documents,
papers, records, of every
past transgression committed
by or against me
blown loose by a stiff wind.

Those books are bullshit,
or maybe they aren't.

I don't have answers.

Maybe they only work if
you're willing to help yourself,
and tonight I am unwilling
as anyone else.

Greasy Handshakes

I don't give a damn
if it's Chuck and Patty's
50th wedding anniversary,
and they booked a booth
or a window table months ago
to celebrate the back leg
of their marathon
with filet mignon, lobster.
Don't give a damn
if Chuck and Patty are
your parents,
or if you made a reservation
for your birthday
because we're your favorite
restaurant in the city,
and you got your suit
dry cleaned for the first time
since your cousin's funeral
after they found him
in his basement apartment
washer fluid blue
with his teeth cutting
through his tongue.
Or if you hired a baby sitter
and this is your first night
together alone since
the baby was born,
and your wife is wearing
high heels and black lingerie
under her dress,
and you booked the date night
suite at the Omni with
a free split of Moet
and chocolate covered strawberries.
A stranger could walk

through the door and shake
my hand with a 100 dollar bill
folded in it and I don't care
who you are, they'll be seated
at your table no questions.
You will have to wait.

Seasonal Unemployment

I buried myself in the old Braddock reservoir
up on the hill, dug a hole in a hole
underneath the rusted shopping carts,
stayed there through the winter
where I ate only egg sandwiches with ketchup,
was visited only by one woman who appeared
during January afternoon whiteouts
with freshly shaved legs.
I emerged in spring after the thaw
to no miracles, no re-birth.
The same eyes, the same blood.
I washed the mud from my hair,
resumed the work as I've always done it,
and waited for the next woman.

Baseball on the Radio

There are moments of peace, though.
Fingernail slivers of hope and contentment.
Just a baseball game coming through the air
like a magic trick on a clear night,
more miraculous than a Kennedy half-dollar
pulled from behind my ear as a child,
the middle of the line-up at bat,
a 1-2 breaking ball in the dirt called
by the announcer whose voice oozes
from the radio speaker like Vaseline,
knowing exactly what that pitch looks like,
that everyone in this country knows, too,
even if they don't really care for the game.

PART THREE

Atom Smasher

One morning we woke and our favorite false idol,
that giant bulb shaped electrostatic nuclear generator
was toppled and laying helpless on the ground.
The developer who owned the land claimed hazard.
The neighborhood kids climbed, tagged it,
the junkies were leaving their dirty needles scattered,
all the rats were migrating to the bar across the street.
But it looked like God reached down and flicked it over.
Maybe that's how it happened and maybe God exists,
angry at our worship of the atom smasher on the hill,
for the reverence we showed for our manmade smokestacks
obscuring the noon sun with fire and soot,
for the bald pride we felt for our industrial might,
and the swing-shift juicers using his name in vain
as they cracked eggs into their morning beers.

Free Doughnut Day

A free doughnut feels like love,
a free dozen more so.
We'd drive, collect one a piece
from every Dunkin'
while the feral dogs who
lived in my parents brains
were thankfully muzzled.

In the front seats
they sang off key to the radio.
My father drank beers,
stashed the crumpled empties
at the feet of my sister and I.
My mother smoked
and flipped her butts out
the open window.

I loved jelly, my sister sprinkles,
my mother maple frosted,
my father cream filled,
all made sweeter by
that magic word. Free.
Because anything you already love
is better when you don't have to pay.

The Meatball

Where do butchers go to dance?
A popsicle stick punchline.

If I love my father, and I think I do,
it's because he is a butcher,
knows what a butcher does.

They get loaded on Budweiser,
play air guitar to the Allman Brothers,

curse at local news stories, their wives,
their children, always have a

quick hundred stashed
for when those children, now adults,

are hurting for cash,
and they give it with creviced hands,

silently cry because they wish it was more,
wish it always had been.

Every month of the year is January
in a windowless meat locker.

They wear wool sweaters through heat waves,
shit blood for days before seeing a doctor,

cure the morning shakes with beer
stashed under their car seats.

One thing they do not do
is fucking dance.

Hot August Night

There's rain, now. I'm a million miles
from 1972 Los Angeles,
the palm trees and low rents.
Never could sing anything, though I tried.
Couldn't wrap my fingers
around a guitar neck to make a pleasant noise.
The world can teach a man
early what his limitations are
and I've been open to the lessons.
I'm not going anywhere today.
No point in unfolding an umbrella.

Four Perch

Four dead perch on a patio table, spines erect.
My catch. A photograph. Me smiling.
My father fileted the fish and
his father pan-fried them on a two-burner
hot plate in butter, salt, and pepper.
We ate the meager pieces no bigger than
Kennedy half-dollars and they drank beers
still lake water cold and said mine were
the tastiest, flakiest fish they had ever eaten.
So young. Fingers too small to hook bait,
not yet a single cavity blossoming rot,
I saw the men I would fight like hell
against but would eventually become.

Boredom

I swam in Turtle Creek,
the water orange from run-off,
surface rainbowed with oil.
Jumped from rocks behind
the Westinghouse plant,
baited hooks with Town Talk
white bread to catch carp,
bullheads, smoked stolen
menthol cigarettes and thumbed
through stolen porno magazines.
Not crying the blues about
nobody having a pool,
too poor for a pool membership,
swimming in pollution.

A friend of mine
used to go to an under 21
dance club in town and chug
bottles of cough syrup,
shoot it back like whiskey.
Another friend spent afternoons
fishing in the town pond,
and smashed the fish with
a hammer until they were
piles of guts rotting in the sun.
A group of us hacked at
a tree with metal beams lifted
from a chain link fence
until we stripped the bark,
left it naked and dead.

Twenty years later and
the tree is alive again.
I see it when I drive here
on nights when I am beached,
nothing better to do but circle
these narrow childhood streets.
The trunk is coated with grey,
leaves sag from its branches
in the humid summers,
the roots grip the earth.
I cannot believe it's alive.
Can't believe it's alive and I still
have nothing better to do
but want to kill it again.

We Used to Love the Mall

I guess this is for my Aunt who used to take me,
patiently listen to my cries for toys,
buy me a scoop of mint chocolate-chip
with an M&M buried in the cone,
hand me pennies to toss in the fountain.

I'm too sentimental. I know this,
but I swear you could find love in the mall.

I watched those Wilkins Township teens
circle the blue ice,
ankles buckle in the rental skates,
while my Aunt fed me egg rolls.
Saw them hold hands in the sweet
air outside the tobacco shop,
loiter in the arcade with no quarters.

Last week there was a sale on snow boots.
I walked the empty concourses,
past the shops permanently gated.
The news stories of gunshots
scared everyone off, even my Aunt
who now shops in the solitude
of her basement on her computer.
Even me. Amazing how after
these years the places I loved most
are the places I can't leave fast enough.

Growing Money

My grandmother put a dollar in a Pringles can
buried it in her closet behind her shoe rack.
She told me, "Money grows. Just wait." A month later
she pulled a ten dollar bill,
a lesson I was supposed to learn.

I've planted money in every corner, in every crack.
Quarters and nickels and dollar bills, but it never bears fruit
just disappears like dried seeds on the hard desert ground,
my pay checks mirages.
She told me that cacti
were bad people who told lies, who committed horrible deeds,
who were condemned to spend eternity in brutal heat
with their arms twisted and broken.

That was years ago, when I was a child.

I wonder if she'd still love me even though
my pockets are empty and I bake, a devil in the sun.

PART FOUR

Poem for Elvis on the Day He Died

Souls are stubborn.
They remain here long after
the flesh turns to dirt.
It's possible to feel them
on my skin the same way
I feel the phantoms
of dead grass scratch my legs,
hear the jazz piano
of an above-ground pool filter
as clear as if I were sitting
in my grandmother's yard.

The Wee Hours

It's the sound that kills me, here.
Like the sound of cotton
sliding on thighs,
the gift of their beauty
old lovers give to new men.

These wee hours
the jukebox weeps sap like a
splintered tree.

Feels like months since
a person walked through
that red door, but soon enough
I know someone will.

A Carton of Smokes, A Gallon of Ice Cream, A Six-Pack

Go down the store.
Pick me up a carton of smokes,
a gallon of Neapolitan ice cream,
a sixer of cold tall-boys.
I eat the chocolate first.
I am a greedy man,
though my needs are simple
and stitched into my DNA.
Like those who came before
my footprints are small,
look for them in the mud that
long ago sucked my shoes off.
Don't burn sage,
read the leaves in the bottom of my mug,
trace my palm lines with your fingers.
My Powerball numbers could hit,
I could find love and marry again.
The overwhelming favorite is
another shift worked,
another day flushed.
The Vegas handicappers know
I am too old to change.
So jot me down on your list.
Bring the items I've asked,
these small trinkets of happiness.

Understanding Bob Seger

All those songs
on the radio impossible
for a young person to understand
when life still projects upward.
To know the songs
one's life must flat-line,
the landscape behind
as even as the highway in front.

I can't tell her this,
even as she talks divorce in
a private moment of confession.
Her voice is railroad spike
echoed and pounded in hard earth,
so I tell her what I can.
No-faults are cheap
and you can't get the paperwork
at the courthouse but rather
a paper goods shop hidden
in a separate office building,
and no lawyer is necessary.

I can't tell her
how the final decree is
a copperhead coiled in the mailbox,
how it will bite no matter
if you've taken a new lover,
or if you think you've
moved on with the help
of the tropical vacation
you took in the immediate
aftermath of the break.

She'll find out as I did,
when she's alone.
We all will understand
sometime what it means
to hear a distant thunderstorm
in the middle of the night,
unable to tell whether
it is approaching or receding.

On Being the Other Man

We're sitting at a sidewalk table talking about little things
that become big things, the tiny annoyances that erode affection,
like the way he leaves half-drunk Coke cans all over the house,
or the way he never folds his clothes, just shoves his shirts
into the dresser drawers in tight, wrinkled balls,
or the way he never buys her favorite dessert
when he stops at the bakery for something sweet.
Maybe, she says, I don't love him enough.
When she says this she looks over her shoulder
at a woman jogging past the café with a leashed dog,
and I search for our waitress so we can get our tab,
walk around the corner to my apartment and lie on my bed,
screens in the windows to let in whatever air is available
so she can forget for awhile
and so I can remember.

To X, in Summer

Summer again and I ignore the moon.
Don't look no matter who elbows my ribs
and points skyward begging me to look
at it pinned there like a donkey tail.
I think of you now and wish I could reach it.
If I could, I'd bash the moon with a stick
until it rips open and rains candy on both of us.

Stuck Inside Swissvale with the Wilmerding Blues Again

All these people I know moved to Swissvale
right after all the good hoagie shops closed,
maybe because all the good hoagie shops closed.

I can see why they're snatching up the houses,
shoeboxes with brick porches and vinyl siding,
because right now the asking prices are low.

Nobody I know is moving to Wilmerding.

Most people just say, "Where's that?"
even though George Westinghouse's castle is there.
Some time ago the town put a sign on Ice Plant Hill
spelling the towns name in white letters like Hollywood.

Wilmerding is not Hollywood, not even Gary, Indiana
or Ashtabula, Ohio just a small town with
a few bars that look like piles of dirty dish rags,
a place where people made air-brakes for trains.

I should move there. It's where I belong.

Johnnie Blue

I've poured it neat,
over one rock or two
with a splash of water
for every CEO in this city,
but never once for myself.

The trade magazines say
Scotland doesn't have
enough single-malt
barreled to keep supply,
that every drop
of 25 year-old increases
in value by the day.

I've never cared
for status symbols.
After a decade waiting tables,
serving drinks, I've acquired
a taste for finer things.
Half empty bottles
of 300 dollar wine
left by guests and consumed
like communion from
coffee mugs, cognac rich
and golden offered as a tip,
left-over foie gras.

After my shift
I drink Johnnie Walker Red,
a double with a splash
of water poured by a bartender
in a Pirates t-shirt
who doesn't need to ask
what it is I want.

In that moment I feel
like royalty, important,
as if all the fine things
in this world sit inches away,
and only cost $4.50.

Long Butts

I should feel good, even grateful
as I leave Shop 'n' Save, bags full
of fresh produce, soft bread baked today,
Hungry Man dinners on sale

Salisbury steak and mashed potatoes,
fried chicken with apple crumb cake
a frozen pizza, a dozen hot wings.

There's a guy by the door sifting through
the ashtray like an archeologist
searching for butts
with a precious drag or two left in them,
menthol or lipstick coated, doesn't matter.

He places them in a Ziplock for later.

Right now, I am a rich man,
a full pack of smokes in my shirt pocket.

I've plenty to give. It hurts.
I walk by praying I'll never
have to smoke used cigarettes.

PART FIVE

Exile on Greensburg Pike

Never been to France, though,
rode motorcycles across the Riviera,
a supermodel's arms around my waist
like Mick Jagger.

Been to Youngstown a few times,
and that town is a giant pot hole.
Not a beach or palm tree in sight,
you don't get laid there.

East Pittsburgh is a maybe at best,
but everyone has gnawed fingernails,
and all the women have boyfriends
who drive monster trucks.

Thanksgiving at Golden Corral

Even though I know better, I am here because
my Grandfather can't roast a turkey and wants
to treat the family to a Thanksgiving dinner.
Can it get better than all-you-can-eat for
twelve dollars and ninety-nine cents?

He's chemo-sick and his fingernails black, rotting.
His sleeves are rolled up to show off his tattoos
done in 1941 when he was thirteen and there was a war
and he was a runaway on a Merchant Marine ship with
a forged baptismal certificate.

He fills his tray with turkey, stuffing, cranberries, potatoes,
only managing to eat half, saving room for pie.
There are so many pies here, apple, pumpkin, cherry.
And he calls the waitress, "Peanut," and asks for coffee,
but they don't smile back.

I could go on about the despair as I eat my baked potato
and breaded chicken wings. Here, where the lonely and obese
line up at the never-ending chocolate fountain. Where toothless
derelicts eat sweet potato mush with their barren wives
and wash it down with Dr. Pepper.

But I won't.

Look at all this food, he says.

My Grandfather believes this is the best life can offer,
an endless bounty at a discounted price.

I will never disagree.

Head on a Platter

Saturday before Christmas and the kitchen is down.
The tickets hang from the printers to the floor.

Every table in the room is full, even the overflow.
I've got two fours, a six, and three deuces

and I have to turn the two fours
into one long nine by eight-thirty.

The air raid sirens blare while buildings burn,
we should all take cover as the bombs fall,

but another server in a panic asks me
to get a dessert order from one of his four-tops.

This server, face has gone red with anxiety,
punches his drink order into the terminal and sprints

back through the dining room squeezing through tables
and dodging guests like an All-American tailback.

So I stop at his four-top and attempt to get an order
and the guy seated in the first position tells me he'd like

his waiter's head on a platter for dessert.
A decade ago one of the old hands pulled me aside,

told me if I expected to be treated with dignity and respect
I should quit and find other work.

That I should always remember who is doing
what on any Saturday night.

They are the ones dining at an expensive restaurant
with their friends and loved ones, taking in a show

or the symphony, or the opera, or a football game.
We are the one's serving them, and the money is all

that matters, we are on the take and we take
everything we can get and if it requires tucking your balls

between your legs to cash in you damn well better do it.
Rather than slap the curly wig off this guy's head,

I can't help but think about how big the tip could be
if I pulled their server into the kitchen and sliced his head

off with one cool, clean sweep of a chef's knife,
placed it on a silver serving tray with scoops of Haagen-Daaz,

chocolate sauce and caramel and whipped cream and walnuts,
and then served it to the table with four spoons and port.

I bet it'd be 50 percent or more in cash, and Jesus help me,
I think it'd be worth it.

The River is Cold Christmas Day

There's a woman I haven't seen
in weeks. She's at a party,
won't see me tonight.

I stand with another woman
on the bank of the Mon.
Eighteen wheelers shake the bridge,
but the water is a corpse.

We kick empty beer cans
into the brush
as the temperature drops
by the minute.

I know she'll hold me when
I start to shiver,
and I'll let her

this the one night a year
I accept charity.

Christmas Day

We stood with our hands
in our pockets waiting for something—
a movie miracle we'd seen on TV,
cotton ball snow, a children's choir singing,
bells ringing for newly winged angels.
None of that happened. Just rain.
Cars with rusted mufflers.
So we turned to the bar to kill the day.

These years later, I know a miracle occurred
even though everyone thinks
spending Christmas on a barstool
is dire as death. They don't know.
They don't understand the gift we exchanged,
our hands touching under the table.
Our warm skin a reminder that
somehow, thankfully, we are not alone.

Sammy's Famous Corned Beef

Soon enough the ball will fall
in Times Square, in Pittsburgh,
and the holiday season will be over.
After all the lights on all
the Christmas trees
are packed away in boxes,
the trees waiting on curbs
like decomposing corpses,
white snow packed into
sheets of ice on sidewalks,
I will celebrate with a case
of post-holiday depression,
not rising from bed until noon,
shivering in front of space heaters
as the gray sky crashes on my head.
Not yet, the weeds are too thick,
so I sit here drinking a beer
in between shifts
to soothe my shaking hands,
to make the dinner turn manageable,
to make the snakes of white
lights constricting around the trees
glow with warmth as the
snow falls in chunks.

Pizza Man

Easter Sunday and I'm in a bar talking about kielbasa
and kishka and sirecz, how there isn't a bakery left
in this city that produces a loaf of paska worth anything.
Pizza Man's not Slovak, but he nods his head, says, "I know."
I don't know if he really does, but that doesn't matter.
Today is the first day in ten years I've called off work.
It feels safe in this place, open for people with no place to go,
or places they don't want to go. Don't know what Pizza Man
is here for. I don't really know him that well, just a friend
of a woman I used to know and I think of her now in
a blue dress, her hair shining like coiled copper on
her father's suburban porch, sitting cross legged on
a wicker chair, sipping a beer from a cooler at her feet.
She didn't know, either, and most who do are long gone,
all the babushkas like my Bubba who waited in line
who walked to the church to receive blessings on their basket
in the Holy Saturday rain, who kneaded the dough,
beat the eggs, hung their sweet cheese wrapped in a dish rag
from a doorknob. Pizza Man orders another round
and I think about the words I said to my Bubba every year,
greeting her at her door as the first-born son.
Christos Voskrese! Christ is Risen!
Indeed, he is.

Bus-Boy Blues
For Bourdain

I am the king of this mountain
of dirty silverware, lipstick stained
wine glasses, heavy white plates
coated with congealed beef tallow, béarnaise.
From the peak I bear witness
to the brutal majesty of an empty dining room,
when, thirty minutes before, the evacuation
swift as an air raid drill for an eight o'clock curtain,
the tables trashed with half-eaten
cheesecake slices and snifters of Sambuca.
Long after the servers cash out
and blow their tips on cheap tequila,
long after the cooks down
enough draft beer and snort enough
to fistfight the whole world,
I will flip the last table with fresh linen,
buff the last glass clear of water spots,
and wander abandoned downtown streets
with only the river rats as my companions.
We will dart from dumpster to dumpster
gnawing on garbage, take refuge under
the al fresco sidewalk tables of the bars,
drag our greasy, black tails over
pavement and brick and concrete,
write our names in piss
on courthouse stones just to show that
for one brief moment, like you,
we were here, we were alive.

PART SIX

Lotto Tickets

Those of us who are the inheritors of empty pockets
wait in convenience store lines armed with
the birthdays of loved ones, digits pulled from
bogus dream books, a strange receipt pattern,
any cluster of numbers that feel lucky on a hunch
for Powerball tickets, our ticket to the good life.

Sometimes there is no hope. Sometimes there is.

My aunt calls and reminds me when the jackpot is high,
tells me if she wins she's going to take care of me,
pay off my student loan debt, my taxes owed,
fix me up with her guy at the Honda dealership
for a new, reliable car before disappearing to
a Caribbean Island like the ones she visited in the 80s.
The crab legs, she says, all you can eat.
So I offer dollar bills to the Commonwealth
knowing the one truth of this life that's been
written in every ancient scripture,
found in the sacred geometry of our city fathers,
in the menstrual cycles of women and the moon:
You can't win if you don't play.

Shelly

I think about them often,
the women in the lobby of the skyscraper where I work,
the ones who appear in dive bar mirrors.
Like Shelly, who wore pastel scrubs
and chain smoked my cigarettes.
She kept talking about her friend who
went missing a few months ago.
I remember seeing his face on posters tacked
on telephone poles around town,
in coffee shop windows asking people
to call if they had any information.
Nobody had any information.
His body was found in the Ohio
downriver, no foul play suspected.
Poor guy probably got drunk
and fell in somewhere on the river walk.

I remember telling an ex
that the universe is indifferent,
there's no good energy or power we
can tap into. We're born. Bad stuff happens.
All of it random, roll of the dice probability.
She wept, and I still feel bad,
but the truth is the truth.
Some 23 year-old kid gets drunk and dies,
how could the universe be anything but?

Shelly kept saying, "I'm sorry, it's over."
Nothing is over for someone lighting
fresh smokes off already lit ones,
so I bought her a beer even though
she had a load of laundry in her car
that'd been there a day, still wet.

She had to go to this guy's house
who had his own machines,
said the sex was average at best,
but whatever was worth it for clean and dry
socks and underwear. I agreed.
Those are the best things in the world.
It was then I told her I had a dryer
in my apartment if she wanted to use it
that night instead. She laughed.

Homeless Man

I should have given him
the cigarette he asked for
because there's no way my night,
bad as it was, was worse than his.

Instead, I belched senseless anger
like a gas bubble in my guts.

I've sought counsel
from therapists
yet never disposed of it,
no matter how many 200 dollar
hours I've rehashed my childhood.

He turned from me,
walked through the alley
where all the restaurant workers
on Sixth Avenue take
smoke breaks, where rats
congregate for their supper.

Should he appear before me
another night, I will fall
to my knees and kiss his feet,
tear at my clothes and beg
for forgiveness though this
display would be another
in a long parade of selfish acts.

Where do I get off
asking to be forgiven by a man
who doesn't have a bed?

Ruin Porn in Spring

I swear it's corn I smell,
the sweetness of the fields.
That's impossible
sitting in a parked car on Dynamo Way
next to concrete trestles
where melting icicles fall
to the cratered pavement
and shatter into disintegrating crystals.
Nothing's been planted,
the wind can't carry that far
except that the wind sometimes does.
I catch a scent
and I run to this valley.

Remember those big fiberglass
slides at every town carnival?
The ones with the dips
you slid down in potato sacks?
During the Pitcairn V.F.D. fair
I climbed to the top and believed
the whole world could be seen,
in reality all I saw was Wall,
its street lights reflecting in the creek.
Or that camp in Deer Valley
where we climbed the look-out
tower on Mt. Davis' peak
where the guide said we could
see Ohio, Maryland, West Virginia?
I am telling the truth
when I say I saw Trafford's
blue water tower in this distance.
No matter where I am
if I look hard enough I see home.

Vinnie Pie

Sometimes, too, I still smell a Vinnie Pie wrapped in paper,
heavy as a Buick, grease bleeding through the cardboard.
In a booth I'd see the old man's gold chains
and Jesus piece hang out from the open buttons
of his white shirt. I'd watch his hands toss the dough
in a flour cloud until it hit the ceiling tile,
where I swear before it fell he'd sneak in a drag
of the cigarette burning in the ashtray beside him
as if he were a circus juggler.

Summer Man

If times are good the beer tastes sweet and crisp,
so cold against my tongue and satisfying I swear
I smell the fresh grass cut and
two-cycle motor oil and gasoline in the air.
If times are bad the beer tastes like pennies,
like rotten apples and exhaust browned snow,
but this morning I woke and felt life in my body.
I can't say for sure how long I'll feel it.

Diner Poem

I keep dreaming about this diner.
Think it was around the back
of the Miracle Mile,
a glass door and a flight of stairs
that led to a dinette and a couple booths,
hot turkey sandwiches and pies
slowly turning in a case.
I never see more than that,
but when I wake I wake happy
and in those first moments
of consciousness I think
I should drive out there for lunch
and be happy for a few hours.
Maybe the diner was in Woolworth's,
or I'm dreaming of the K-Mart
lunch counter where I ate hamburgers
while my grandfather filled
an ashtray and flirted with Bonnie,
who kept his coffee cup full.
That probably wasn't her name,
and to be honest I'm not sure this ever happened.

Perfection

Driving Rt. 48 I see the Lokay Lanes sign
celebrating a 300 game and I am filled with longing.
Never have I done anything the best it can be done;
the feat must feel like the first big winter snow
where new lovers shut themselves indoors
stay in bed while white piles in inches on power lines.
I cannot despair. The Mr. Tire mechanic knows
perfection, an oil change under thirty minutes,
so do broiler cooks pumping out perfect
medium rare steaks on New Year's Eve.
It's the way Incas fit stones together with no mortar.
It's there, always right in front of us,
ripe plums hanging from low branches
easy to grasp, not even a 300 game,
but the way a lover rests her feet on my lap.
Perfection can be found anywhere,
so long as we let it lean in and kiss us.

Sometimes Waiting Tables Feels Like This

We have this 400 dollar night,
our bills paid in five hours,
and every packet of Splenda,
Equal faces the same direction
in all the sugar caddies.

Let's clock out and hang-glide
to the bar feeling rich
as railroad tycoons in top-hats,
and for the next hour
kiss each other's forehead
with dedicated purpose,

knowing that phone vibrating
in your purse can answer
any question we ask,
so let's ask it now,
"Does it get better than this?"
though we know the answer.

PART SEVEN

Frank Sinatra Playing on the Jukebox, 2016

My cigarette cherry is a radio tower's light blinking
emergency broadcasts. Please don't touch the dial.

ACKNOWLEDGEMENTS

Thanks to the editors of the following magazines where some of these poems appeared (sometimes with different titles and in different forms). *Barrelhouse (online), Blue Mountain Review, Chiron Review, Edison Literary Review, Fried Chicken and Coffee, Gulf Coast, Melancholy Hyperbole, Pittsburgh Post-Gazette, Poetry Breakfast, Rising Phoenix Review, Sandy River Review, Uppagus,* and *Low Ghost Press' Unconditional Surrender: An Anthology of Love Poems.*

Thanks to Bob Pajich and Zigeller Boy Press, where a number of these poems were published in my chapbook, *Moons Over My Hammy* (Zigeller Boy, 2018).

Special thanks to Ben Gwin, Bob Pajich (again), T.C. Jones, S.J. Guzik, Lori Jakiela, Dave Newman, Scott Silsbe, Jason Baldinger, Kris Collins, Taylor Grieshober, Hillary Roman, and all my co-workers.

ABOUT THE AUTHOR

Richard L. Gegick is from Trafford, PA. He is the author of *Moons Over My Hammy* (Zigeller Boy, 2018). He's worked in restaurants for over twelve years, and his poems and short stories have appeared in numerous periodicals including *Hot Metal Bridge, Burrow Press Review, Chiron Review,* and *Gulf Stream.* He lives in Pittsburgh where he writes and waits tables in a high-end steakhouse.

CPSIA information can be obtained
at www.ICGtesting.com
Printed in the USA
LVHW110948080121
676059LV00009B/28

9 780578 537726